DENES AGAY'S
LEARNING TO PLAY
PIANO
BOOK 1
GETTING STARTED!

Order No. AM998921

Compiled and edited by Denes Agay.
Associate Editor: Nancy Bachus.
Music processed by Paul Ewers.
Designed and art directed by Michael Bell Design.
Illustrated by Jon Burgerman.
Printed in the EU.

ISBN: 978-1-84938-298-4

Visit Hal Leonard Online at
www.halleonard.com

Contact us:
Hal Leonard
7777 West Bluemound Road
Milwaukee, WI 53213
Email: info@halleonard.com

In Europe, contact:
Hal Leonard Europe Limited
42 Wigmore Street
Marylebone, London, W1U 2RY
Email: info@halleonardeurope.com

In Australia, contact:
Hal Leonard Australia Pty. Ltd.
4 Lentara Court
Cheltenham, Victoria, 3192 Australia
Email: info@halleonard.com.au

POSITION AT THE PIANO

● Sit with a straight back facing the middle of the keyboard – leaning very slightly forward.

● Feet should be on the floor. A footstool or box can be used if feet do not reach the floor.

● Allow the upper arm to hang loosely. Adjust seat so that elbow, wrist and hand are at the height of the keyboard.

HAND POSITION

● Hands are cupped with palms down as if holding a small, round object like a ball.

● Fingers are curved, with the fleshy part, not the nails, touching the keys.

FINGER NUMBERS

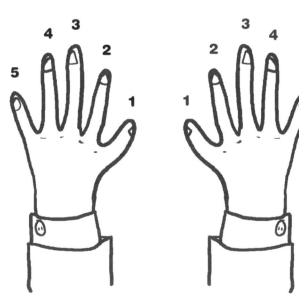

● When playing the piano our fingers have numbers. The thumb is the first finger in each hand.

● Practise the finger numbers this way:
Hold your hands in front of you as shown above, fingers spread, and wiggle each finger as its number is called out by your teacher.

At first, practise this separately with each hand, then with the two hands together.

THE KEYBOARD

The piano has white keys and black keys. The white keys are in a
row touching each other. The black keys are raised and arranged in groups
of twos and threes.

● Draw a circle around all groups of two black keys on this keyboard:

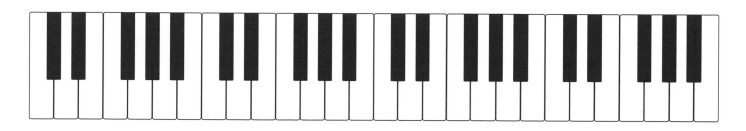

● Make a loose fist – raise your hand and 'fall' on the group of
two black keys with a loose wrist. (Do this with each hand individually.)

● Put the middle (third) finger of both hands on neighbouring
black keys in the 'two-black key' group. Play and sing this little song.
(Your teacher will show you how.)

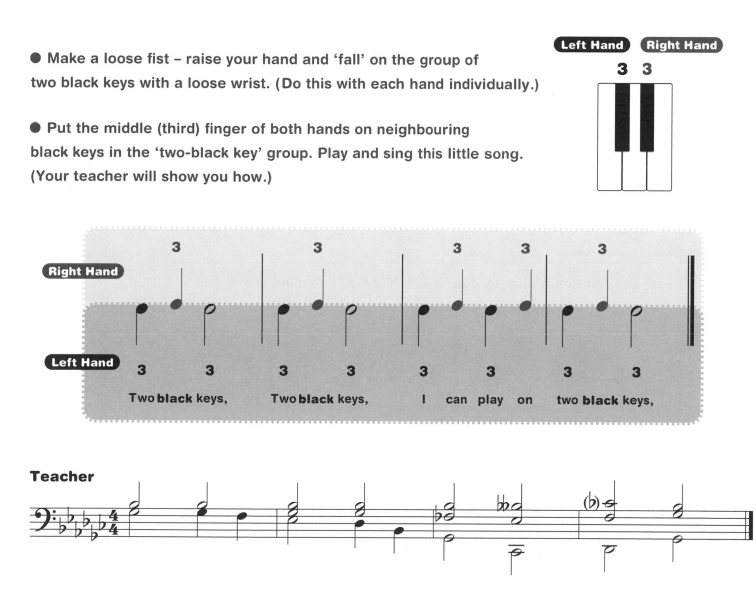

Teacher

● Place the middle (third) finger of your left hand on a black key in the 'three-black key' group
and play a melody of your own invention to fit these words. (Sing the words as you play.)

'Three black keys, Three black keys, I can play on three black keys'

● Now place the middle finger of your right hand on one of the three black keys and play another
melody to fit the same words.

DIRECTIONS ON THE KEYBOARD

Each key, white or black, produces a different note.

Going to the left, or going down the keyboard, notes gradually become lower.

Going to the right, or going up the keyboard, notes become gradually higher.

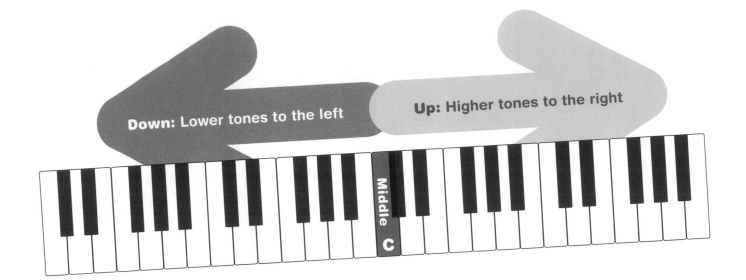

Down: Lower tones to the left

Up: Higher tones to the right

● Place the middle (third) finger of your right hand on **Middle C** and play eight white keys, going higher step-by-step.

● Repeat with the left hand, playing down from **Middle C**, singing the words.

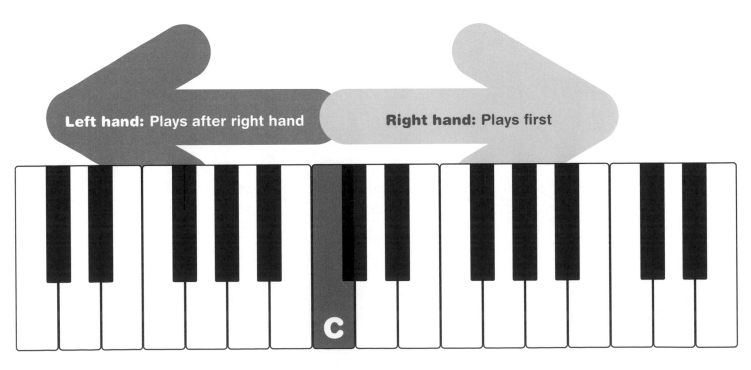

Left hand: Plays after right hand

Right hand: Plays first

C

er - low   ing - go   we're left   the To   To the   right we're   go - ing   high - er

PLAYING BY FINGER NUMBERS
with the three middle fingers 2-3-4

● Put your two hands on the keyboard in this position.

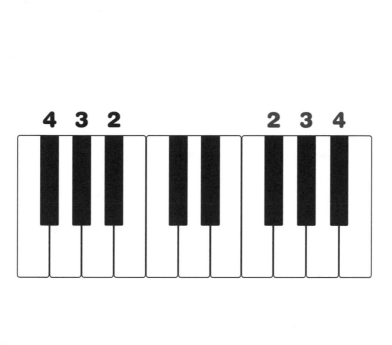

Merrily We Roll Along

● Play and sing:

Observe that the finger numbers follow the rise and fall of the melody.
Words underlined are held twice as long as the other words.
(Such combinations of long and short notes give music its patterns of rhythm.)

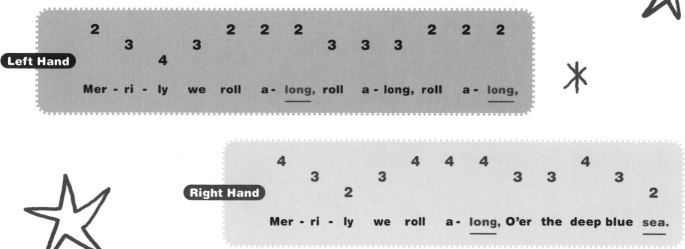

Left Hand

2				2	2	2			2	2	2
	3		3				3	3	3			
		4										

Mer - ri - ly   we roll a- long, roll   a - long, roll   a - long,

Right Hand

4				4	4	4			4		
	3		3				3	3		3	
		2									2

Mer - ri - ly   we roll   a - long, O'er the deep blue sea.

7

MORE PLAYING BY FINGER NUMBERS
with all five fingers

Place your hands on the keyboard as shown on this chart.

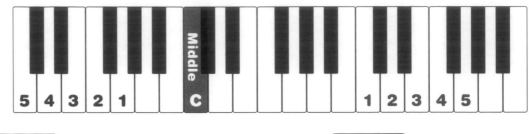

Middle C

5 4 3 2 1   1 2 3 4 5

Left Hand Finger numbers   **Right Hand** Finger numbers

With each hand separately, using all fingers as shown by the finger numbers:

1. First, play 'in the air.'

2. Then, tap on the keys.

3. Finally, play these melodies, stepping from one white key to its neighbour and calling out the finger numbers.

4. Always press down the keys gently but firmly; fingers should maintain their curved position.

Left Hand

1   2   3   4   5 - 5   4   3   2   1

Right Hand

5   4   3   2   1 - 1   2   3   4   5

Here is another melody you can play by the finger numbers.

Here We Go
Use the same position on the keyboard as above.
(Underlined words are held twice as long as the others.)

Left Hand

5   4   3   4   3   2   3   2   1   2   3   4   5

Here we go, Here we go, To the top and down we go.

1. Sing out the numbers as you play.

2. Sing the words.

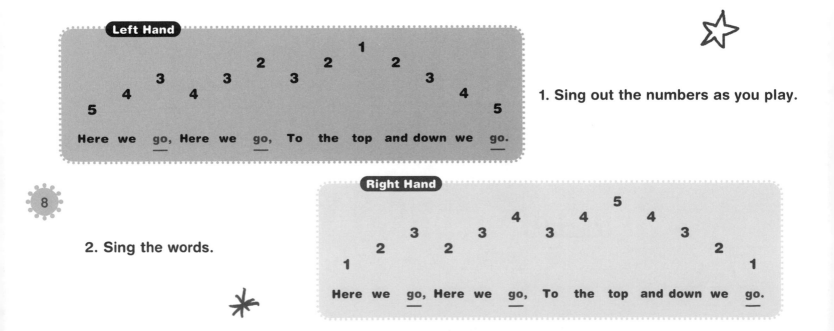

Right Hand

1   2   3   2   3   4   3   4   5   4   3   2   1

Here we go, Here we go, To the top and down we go.

SHORT & LONG NOTES
Note Values

● Sing 'Here We Go' again and this time, instead of playing, clap your hands as you sing.

Clap	X	X	X	X	X	X	X	X	X	X	X	X	X	X	X	X
Sing	Here	we	go,		Here	we	go,		to	the	top	and	down	we	go.	

Did you notice that every time you sang the word 'go' you clapped your hands twice, while singing the other words you clapped only once?

This means that the note sung to the word 'go' is held twice as long as the notes sung to the other words; it receives two counts while the other words receive one count.

This is a one-count note and is called a **crotchet** (or quarter-note).

This is a two-count note and is called a **minim** (or half-note).

This is a four-count note and is called a **semibreve** (or whole-note).

To make reading notes easier, we divide music into **bars** (or measures) with **barlines**
There is a **double barline** at the end of the piece.

Sing the following melody and clap your hands in rhythm to every beat.

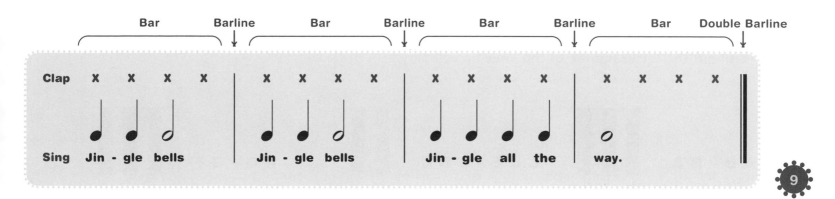

9

THE MUSICAL ALPHABET

The white keys of the piano are named after the first seven letters of the alphabet:

A B C D E F G

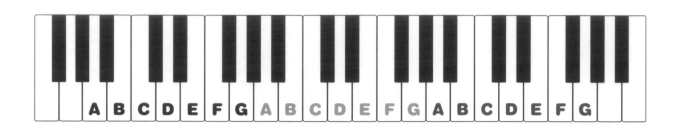

Observe that after **G** the letter names start again with **A**.

(**A** is the white key to the left of the third black key.)

● You already know the location of the **Middle C**.

Now play all **C**s (to the left of the two black keys) from the lowest to the highest.

How many **C**s are on your keyboard? ....

● Play all **D**s from the highest to the lowest. How many **D**s are there? ....

● Similarly locate and play all...

        Es (to the right of the two black keys)

        Fs (to the left of the three black keys)

        Bs (to the right of the three black keys)

        Gs (between the first and second of the three black keys)

        As (between the second and third of the three black keys)

● Play these keys all over the keyboard.

(Call out the letter names of the keys as you play.)

A B – B A   C D E – E D C   F G – G F

● Write the letter names on the keys marked **X**.

Play them (with any finger) as you call out the letter names.

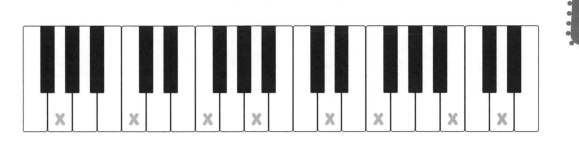

PLAYING BY LETTER NAMES
& FINGER NUMBERS

● Place the first finger of the right hand on **Middle C** and play this melody, calling out the letter names.

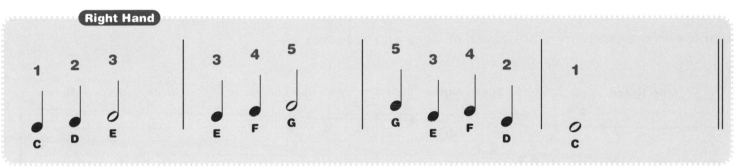

● Place the fifth finger of the left hand on **A** below **Middle C** and play this melody as you call out the letter names.

● Play this melody. Do you recognise the tune?

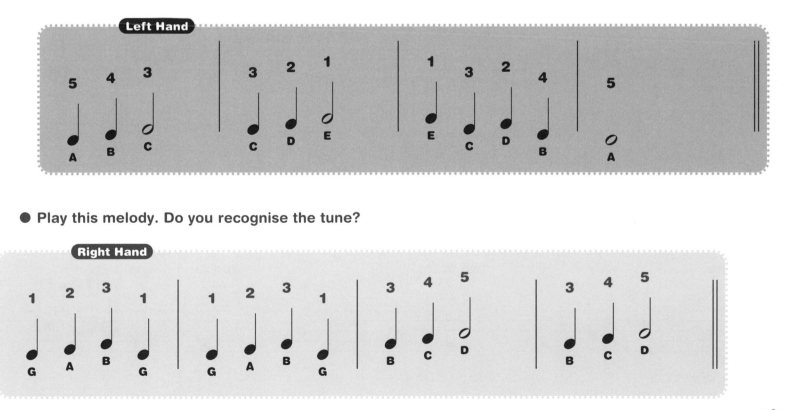

● With the third finger of either hand play those keys whose letter names are called out by your teacher, one by one.

THE STAVE

You have seen that the notes follow the rise and fall of the melody.
In order to see exactly how high or low a note is, we need some guidelines.

These guidelines are called **the stave**, a system of five lines and
four spaces, numbered from the bottom up.

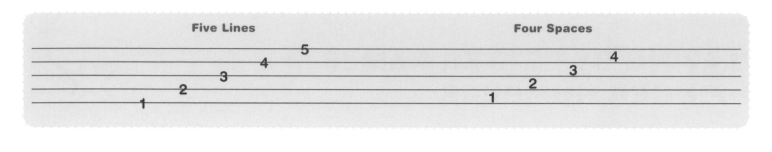

● Notes on the stave are placed both on lines and in spaces

Line Notes	Space Notes	Write four Line Notes	Write four Space Notes

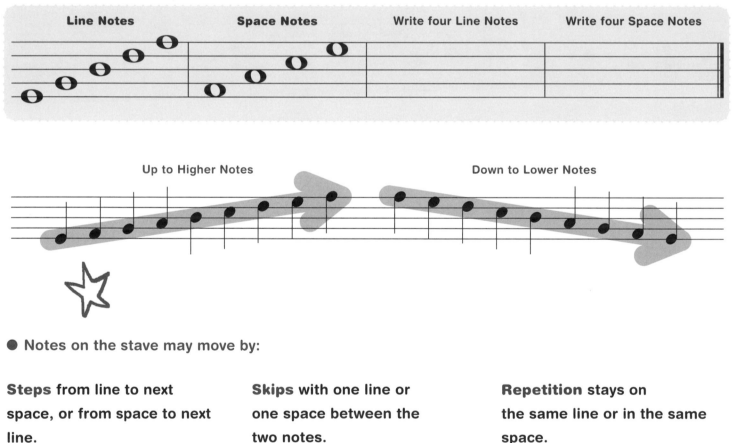

● Notes on the stave may move by:

Steps from line to next space, or from space to next line.

Play neighbour white keys with neighbour fingers.

Skips with one line or one space between the two notes.

Skip one white key and skip a finger.

Repetition stays on the same line or in the same space.

Played on the same key using the same finger.

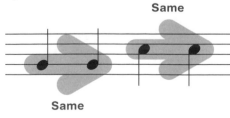

THE GRAND STAVE

For piano music two staves are used: the **treble stave** and the **bass stave**.

The **treble stave**, headed by the **treble clef**, is for higher notes, usually played by the right hand.

The **bass stave**, headed by the **bass clef**, is for lower notes, usually played by the left hand (observe the dots above and below the fourth line).

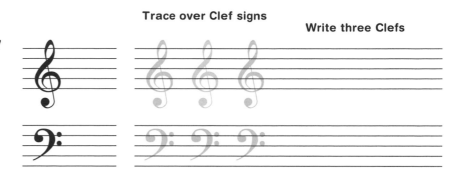

Trace over Clef signs

Write three Clefs

The two staves, connected by a line and a **brace** are called the **grand stave**.

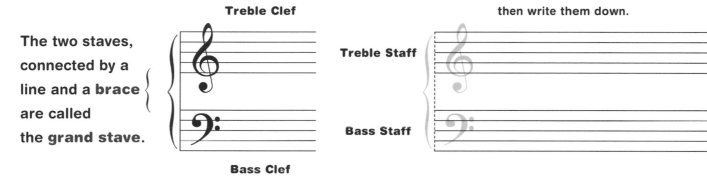

Treble Clef

Bass Clef

Treble Staff

Bass Staff

Trace over the Brace, Line, and Clefs: then write them down.

You have seen that music is divided by **barlines** into **bars** (or measures). Barlines are drawn on the grand stave too. Usually each bar has the same number of beats (counts), as indicated by the **time signatures**.

TIME SIGNATURE $\frac{2}{4}$

The upper number (in this case **2**) tells us how many counts there are in a **bar** (two).

The lower number (**4**) shows what kind of note receives one count (**crotchet**).

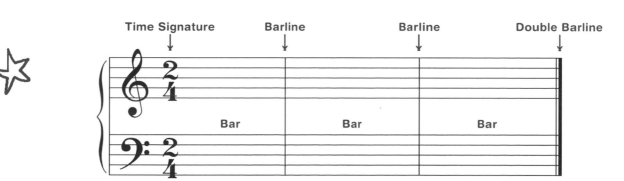

Time Signature   Barline   Barline   Double Barline

Bar   Bar   Bar

Whenever the lower number is 4 in a time signature, a crotchet receives one count.

$$\frac{2}{4} = \frac{2}{\text{♩}}$$

MIDDLE C ON THE STAVE

Middle C is on a line of its own between the two staves.

When played by the right hand, **Middle C** is written closer to the **treble stave**, just below the first line.

When played by the left hand, **Middle C** is written closer to the **bass stave**, just above the fifth line.

Clap

Count   1   2   1   2   1   2   1   2   1   2   1   2   1   2   1   2

C   C   Mid - dle   C   C   C   plain to   see.

Practice Directions:

1. Clap your hands for every note, counting aloud the proper number of beats in each bar.
2. Play the notes and call out the letter names.
3. Play the notes and count aloud the beats in each bar.
4. Play the notes and sing the words.

SKILL BUILDER: Try playing other **C**s with your third finger.

NOTES AROUND MIDDLE C

In every piece:

● First, play and sing the letter names.

● Then play and count.

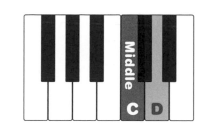

Right Hand

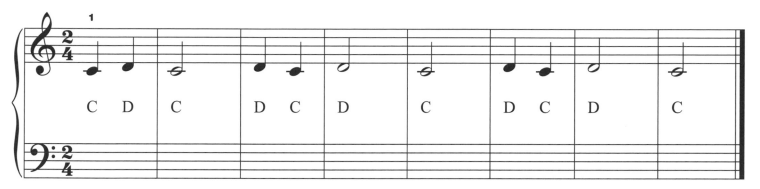

C D C   D C D   C   D C D   C

Count   1   2   1   2

Teacher

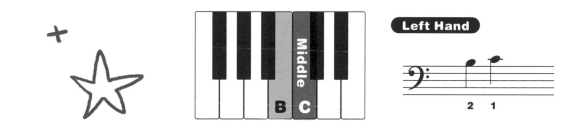

Left Hand

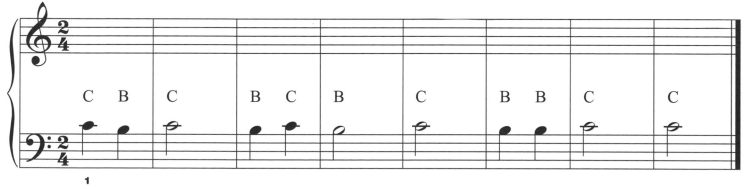

C B C   B C B   C   B B C   C

Count   1   2   1   2

Teacher

SKILL BUILDER: Play also with fingers **2–3–2** and **3–4–3**. (Play with firm nail joints.)

Play in other octaves.

Play other **B**s and **D**s all over the keyboard.

Three-Note Jig

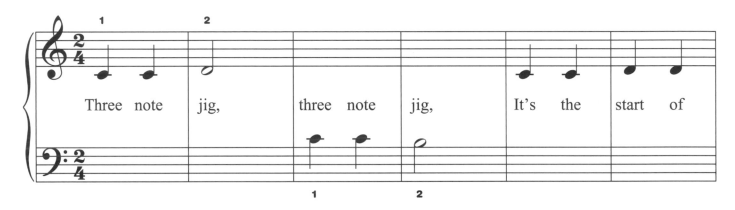

Three note jig, three note jig, It's the start of

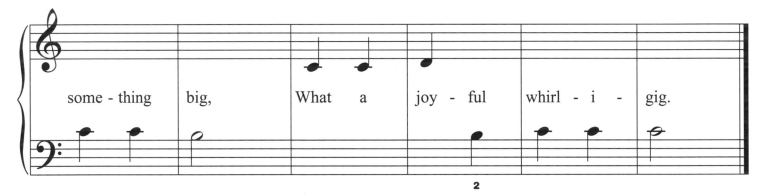

some - thing big, What a joy - ful whirl - i - gig.

Teacher

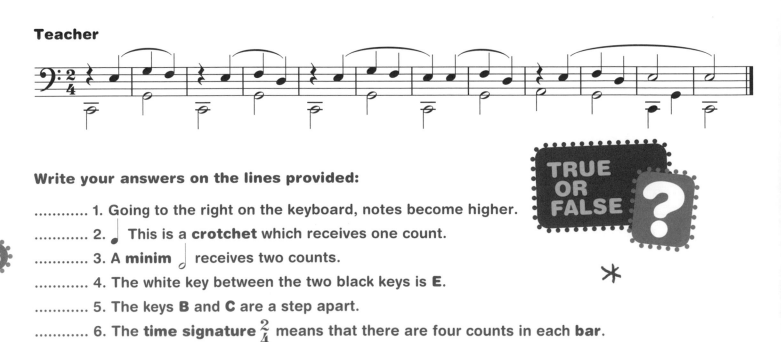

Write your answers on the lines provided:

.... 1. Going to the right on the keyboard, notes become higher.

.... 2. ♩ This is a **crotchet** which receives one count.

.... 3. A **minim** ♩ receives two counts.

.... 4. The white key between the two black keys is **E**.

.... 5. The keys **B** and **C** are a step apart.

.... 6. The **time signature** $\frac{2}{4}$ means that there are four counts in each **bar**.

16

INTERVALS

The distance between two notes or two keys is called an **interval**.

Intervals are measured and named according to the number of notes or keys involved.

In measuring intervals we count all the notes;
the two notes of the interval *and* the notes (white keys) between the two.

THE 2ND (SECOND): LIKE A STEP

ON THE KEYBOARD

A **2nd** is the distance from one white key to the next white key, up or down.

ON THE STAVE

A **2nd** is the distance from a line to the next space, or from a space to the next line.

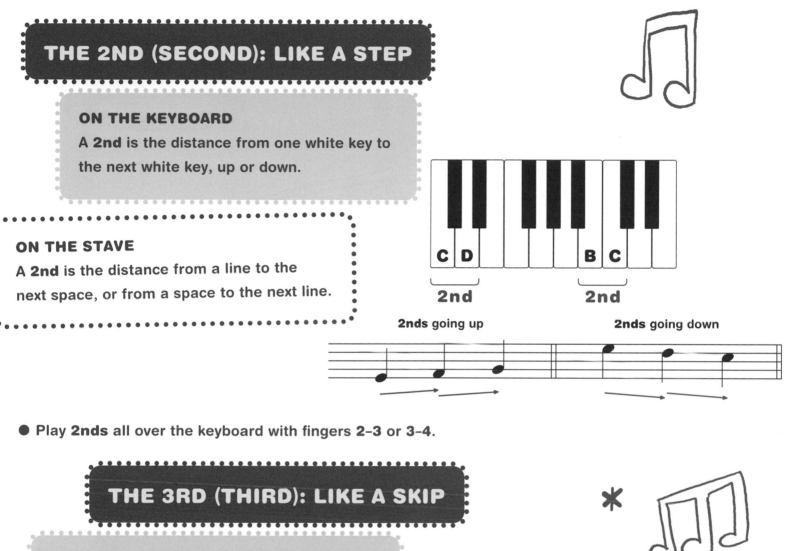

● Play **2nds** all over the keyboard with fingers **2–3** or **3–4**.

THE 3RD (THIRD): LIKE A SKIP

ON THE KEYBOARD

A **3rd** is the distance between two white keys with one white key in between them.

ON THE STAVE

A **3rd** is the distance from a line to the next line, or from a space to the next space.

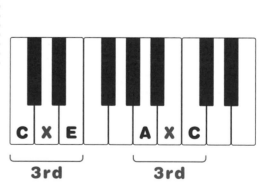

● Play **3rds** all over the keyboard with fingers **1–3**, **2–4** and **3–5**.

SKILL BUILDER: Close your eyes and play **2nds** and **3rds** with different finger combinations.

NEW TIME SIGNATURE:

4/4 Four counts to a Bar (measure).
A **Crotchet** (quarter-note) ♩ gets one count.

NEW NOTE:

E on the first line of the treble stave
(a skip above **Middle C**)

B C D E

Right Hand   1 2 3

Left Hand

2 1

My Model Train

● Play other **Es** on the keyboard.

● How many **Es** are in this piece?

● Find and circle the **3rd** in this piece.

Up   the   track   up   and   back,   lit - tle   trains   go   fast;

Count   1   2   3   4   etc.

It's   out   race,   keep   the   pace,   please   don't   come   in   last.

18

Teacher

The Willow Tree

● How many **3rds** (skips) are in this piece?

● How many **2nds** (steps)?

Wil - low, how you swing and sway;

Un - der you I love to play.

Teacher

Play every piece at least three times:

1. Play and sing the letter names.
2. Play and count the beats.
3. Play and sing the words.

(Always listen for a beautiful tone.)

NEW NOTE:

A on the fifth line of the **bass stave**

(a skip below **Middle C**)

Rain, Go Away

● Play **A**s throughout the keyboard.

● How many **A**s are in this piece?

Rain please | go a - way, | I don't like this | wea - ther;

When there's sun | then it's fun, | Friends play to - ge - ther.

Teacher

stacc.

20

The A-C-E Song

● Point out all **3rds** to your teacher.

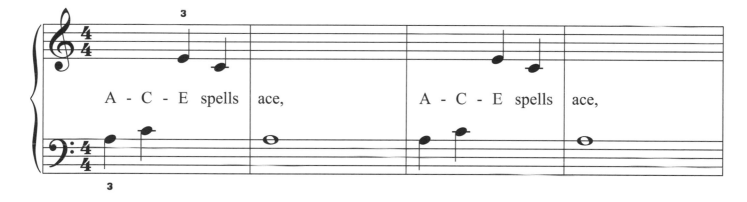

A - C - E spells ace,   A - C - E spells ace,

D - B - D and   C - A - C   just   stare right in your   face

Teacher

NEW NOTE VALUE

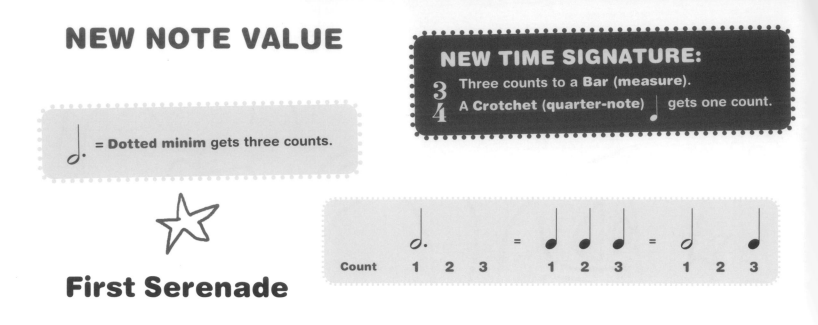

NEW TIME SIGNATURE:

3/4 Three counts to a Bar (measure).
A Crotchet (quarter-note) ♩ gets one count.

♩. = Dotted minim gets three counts.

Count 1 2 3 = 1 2 3 = 1 2 3

First Serenade

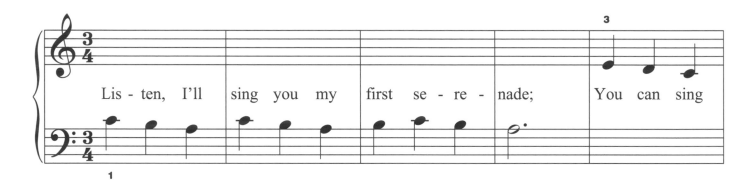

Lis - ten, I'll sing you my first se - re - nade; You can sing

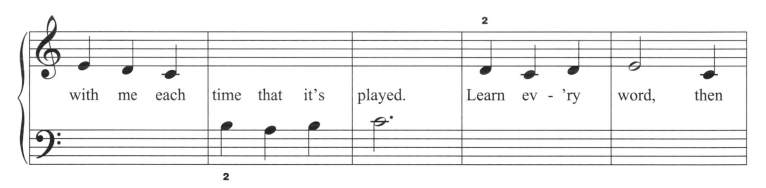

with me each time that it's played. Learn ev - 'ry word, then

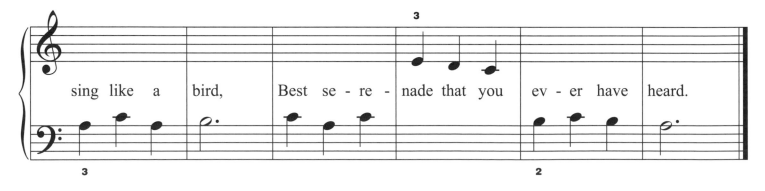

sing like a bird, Best se - re - nade that you ev - er have heard.

Teacher

Reluctant Sleepy Head

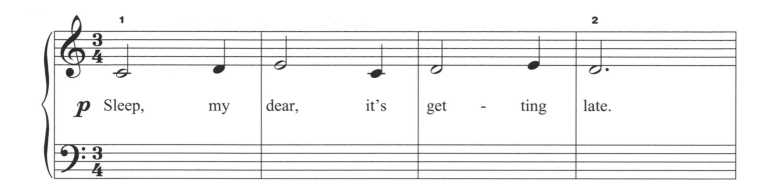

Sleep, my dear, it's get - ting late.

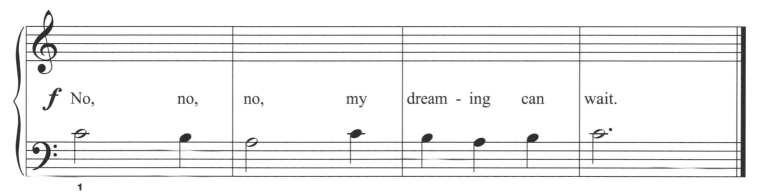

No, no, no, my dream - ing can wait.

Repeat this piece playing the right-hand part
an octave (eight keys) higher, and the left-hand
part an octave lower.

p = Piano = soft
f = Forte = loud

The Evening Bell

Optional teacher-student duet:

1. Student plays only **bass** or **treble part**.
2. Student may use both hands, playing **octaves**.
3. Vary dynamics and tone quality.

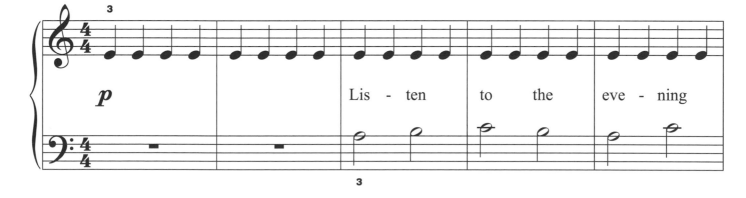

Lis - ten to the eve - ning

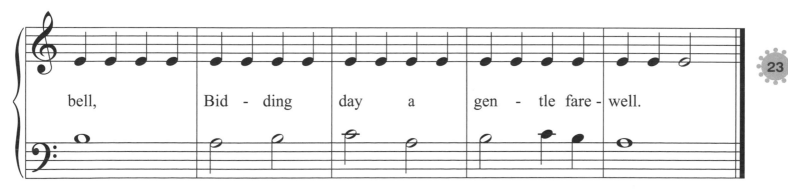

bell, Bid - ding day a gen - tle fare - well.

● Play **Gs** (and then **Fs**) throughout the keyboard.

Move in an arc ⌒ when jumping octaves.

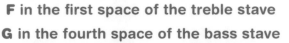

Our Flag

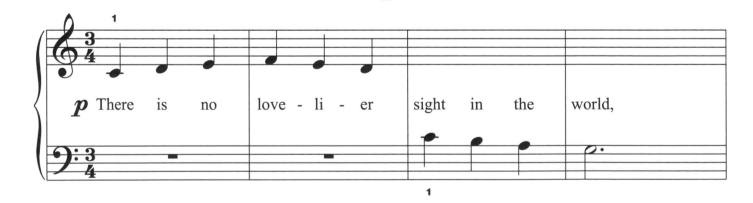

p There is no love - li - er sight in the world,

f Look at our flag as it waves when un - furled!

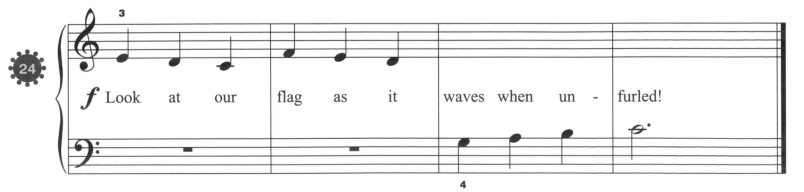

24

Yankee Doodle

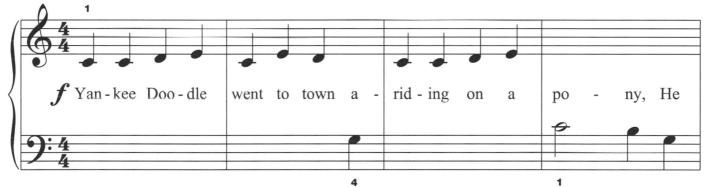

f Yan-kee Doo-dle went to town a - rid-ing on a po - ny, He

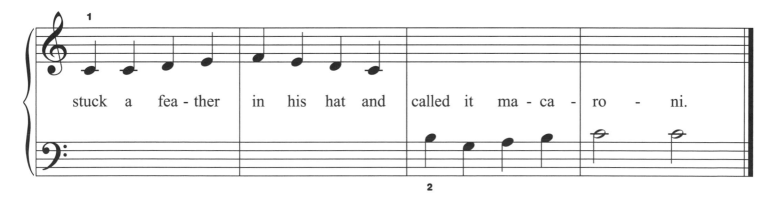

stuck a fea-ther in his hat and called it ma-ca-ro - ni.

Teacher

NEW INTERVAL: THE 4th

ON THE KEYBOARD
A **4th** is the distance between two white keys with two keys in between them (**X X**).

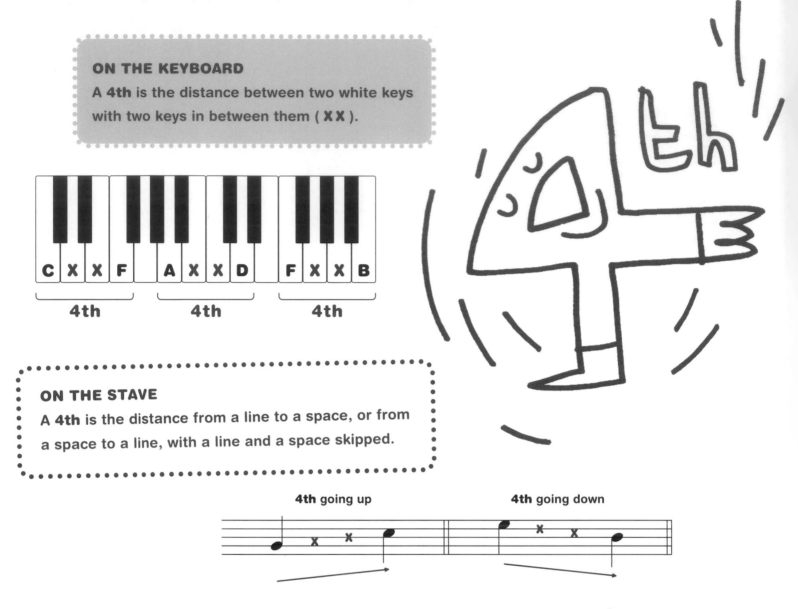

C	X	X	F		A	X	X	D		F	X	X	B

4th   4th   4th

ON THE STAVE
A **4th** is the distance from a line to a space, or from a space to a line, with a line and a space skipped.

4th going up   **4th** going down

● Play **4ths**, up and down, all over the keyboard with fingers **1–4** and **2–5**.

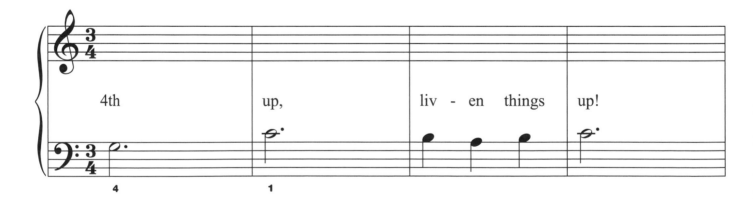

4th   up,   liv - en   things   up!

4th   down,   jump   like   a   clown!

OCTAVE SIGN *8va/8vb*

The symbol *8va* and a dotted line over the notes *8va* ____ mean that you play these notes an octave (eight keys) higher.

The symbol *8vb* and a dotted line under the notes *8vb* ____ mean that you play these notes an octave (eight keys) lower.

Polka Time

- Circle all **4ths** in this piece.
- How many **3rds** are there?
- How many **2nds**?

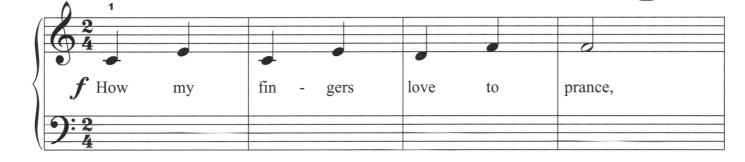

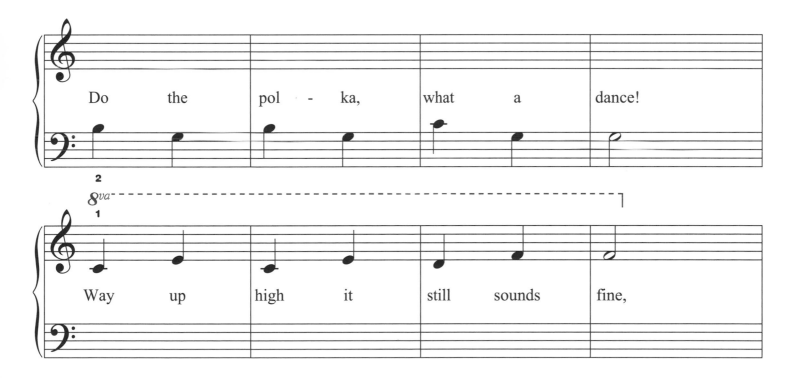

f How my fin - gers love to prance,

Do the pol - ka, what a dance!

Way up high it still sounds fine,

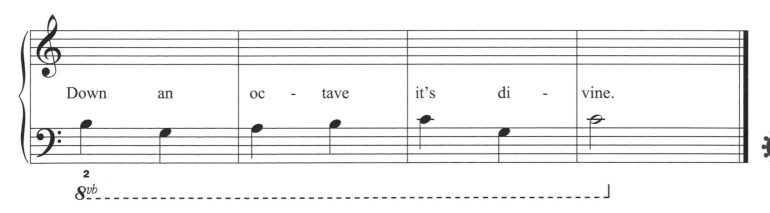

Down an oc - tave it's di - vine.

The **treble clef** is also called the **G clef** because its graceful design curls around the second line of the treble stave where the G above Middle C is located.

The **bass clef** is also called the **F clef** because its design originates on the fourth line of the bass stave where F below Middle C is located.

Notice that the two dots of the F clef surround the F line.

NEW NOTE   NEW NOTE

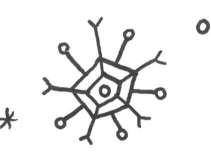

G Clef

G

F

F Clef

WARM UP IN 6/4 TIME

6 Six counts to each **Bar (measure)**.
4 **Crotchet (quarter-note)** gets one count.

● Circle all **Fs** and **Gs**.

● Play this piece and call out the letter names of the notes.

● Then play it again and count aloud the beats in each bar.

● Then play it and sing the words.

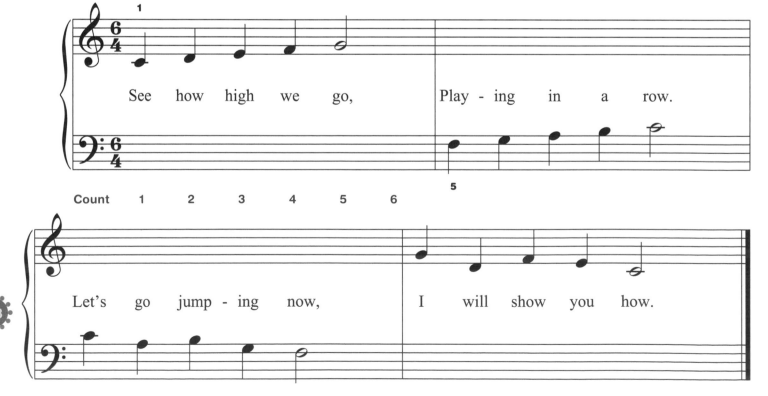

See how high we go,   Play - ing in a row.

Count   1   2   3   4   5   6

Let's go jump - ing now,   I will show you how.

Play this piece four ways:

● Play as written.

● Play the left-hand part as written and the right-hand part an octave higher.

● Play the right-hand part as written and the left-hand part an octave lower.

● Play the right-hand part an octave higher and the left-hand part an octave lower.

Snowflakes

Use the same hand position as you did on page 28.

p Swirl - ing and twirl - ing the snows are un - furl - ing. They

melt down the pane like a sil - ver - y rain.

TECHNIQUE HINT:

When the two hands play together, each one playing a different note, make sure that the finger of the left hand and the finger of the right hand strike the keys exactly together.

I'm Waltzing!

Use the same hand position as you did on page 28.

● Circle all **4ths**.

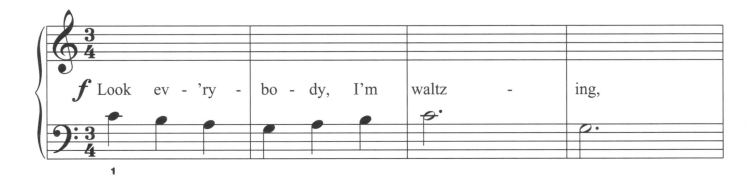

f Look ev - 'ry - bo - dy, I'm waltz - ing,

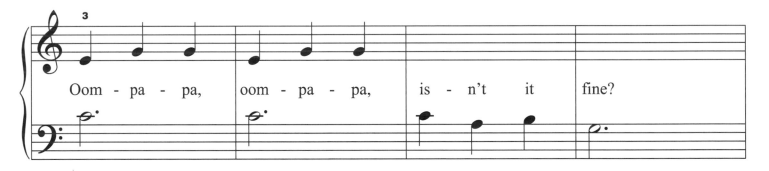

Oom - pa - pa, oom - pa - pa, is - n't it fine?

Join in the fun, be my part - ner,

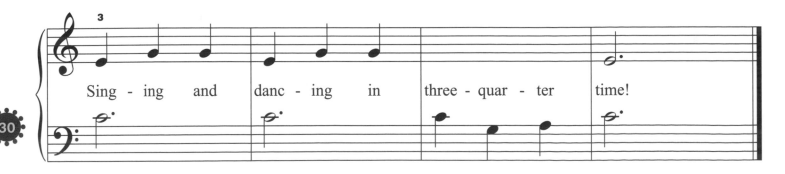

Sing - ing and danc - ing in three - quar - ter time!

NEW INTERVAL: THE 5th

ON THE KEYBOARD

A **5th** is the distance between two white keys with three white keys in between them (**X X X**).

ON THE STAVE

A **5th** is the distance from a line to a line, or from a space to a space, with one line and two spaces, or one space and two lines, skipped.

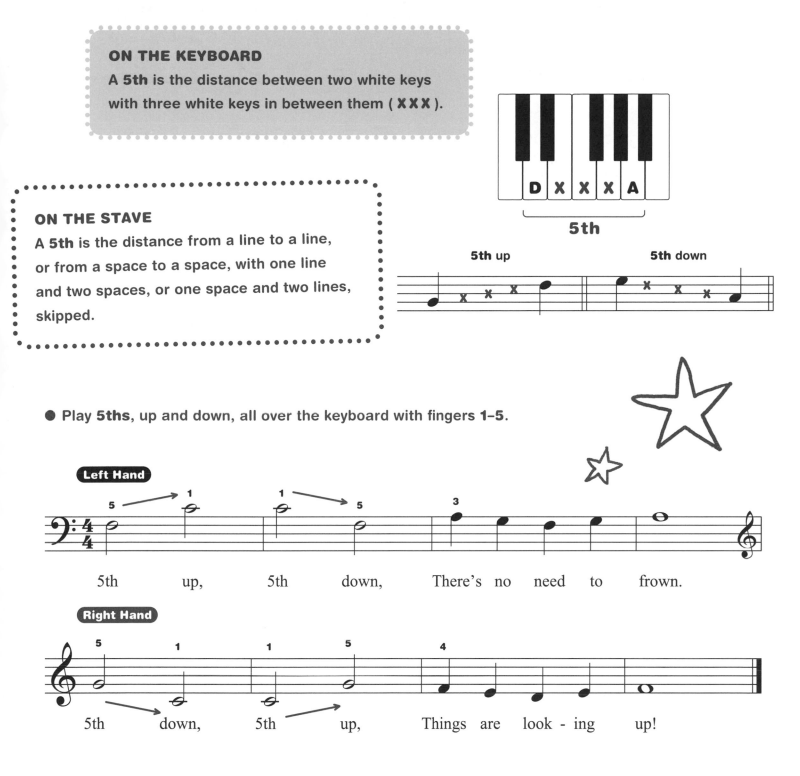

● Play **5ths**, up and down, all over the keyboard with fingers **1–5**.

Left Hand

5th   up,   5th   down,   There's no need to frown.

Right Hand

5th   down,   5th   up,   Things are look - ing up!

Hop Scotch

31

Rest signs indicate periods of silence in music.

This sign, a little beam hanging from the fourth line, is called a **semibreve rest**.

It indicates silence in one whole **bar** (measure) of any kind.

Early Morning

Use the same hand position as you did on page 28.

● Circle the **5ths** in this piece.

● How many **3rds** are there?

Ear - ly morn-ing sun - shine, ear - ly morn-ing dew;

What a love-ly day, I'll spend it all with you.

Teacher

> **Tempo** is the rate of speed at which a piece of music is performed.
> It is important to play a piece at a tempo that fits its mood and character.
> You will find a **tempo mark** at the beginning of most pieces.

The Wind And The Breeze

Use the same hand position as you did on page 28.

Slowly

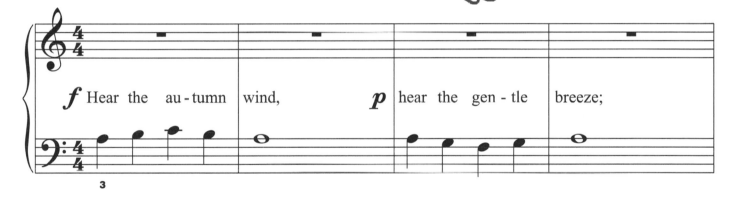

f Hear the au-tumn wind,   *p* hear the gen-tle breeze;

f Au-tumn wind, blow hard,   *p* breeze, ca-ress the trees.

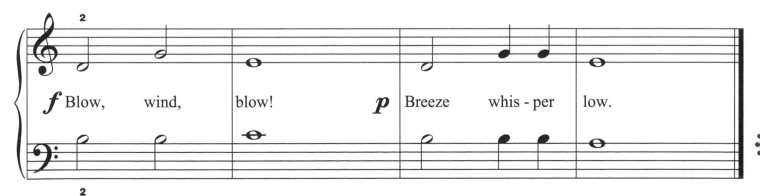

f Blow, wind, blow!   *p* Breeze whis-per low.

Camping Trip

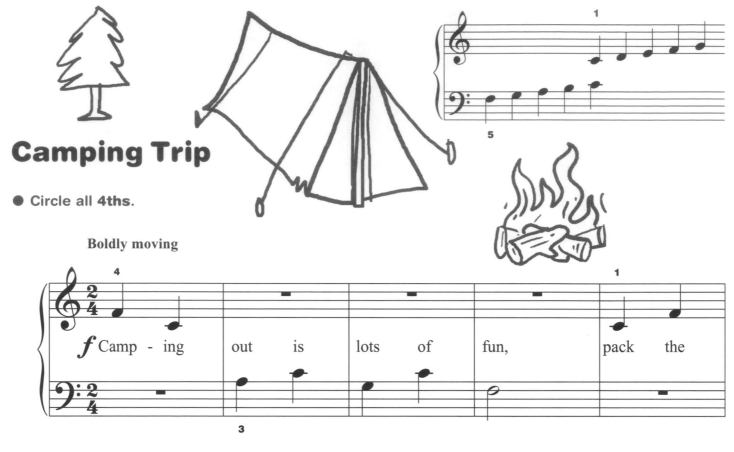

● Circle all **4ths**.

Boldly moving

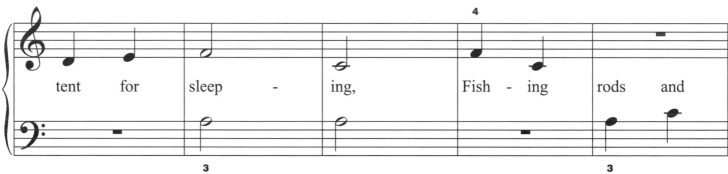

f Camp - ing   out   is   lots   of   fun,   pack   the

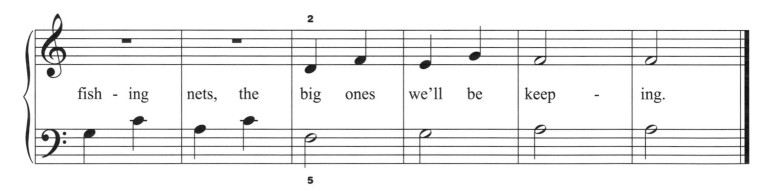

tent   for   sleep - ing,   Fish - ing   rods   and

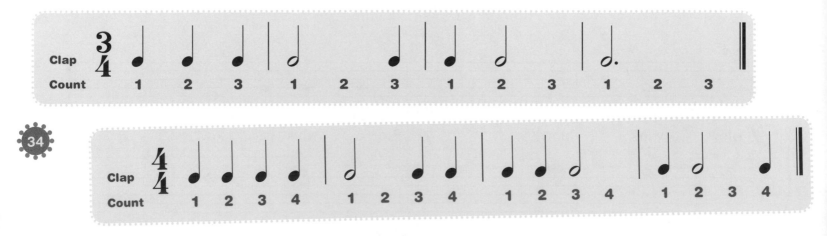

fish - ing   nets, the   big   ones   we'll   be   keep -   ing.

● Count the beats and clap once for each note in the following exercises:

Clap **3/4** | | | | | | | | | | | |
Count 1   2   3 | 1   2   3 | 1   2   3 | 1   2   3

Clap **4/4** | | | | | | | | | | | | | | |
Count 1   2   3   4 | 1   2   3   4 | 1   2   3   4 | 1   2   3   4

34

REVIEW

● Write the indicated whole notes on the stave below.

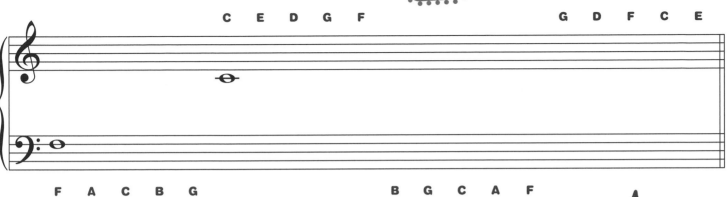

● What words do these notes spell out? Write in the letter names.

● Write in the counts, and put in the missing barlines.

Count   1   2

Count   1   2   3   4

Count   1   2   3

C POSITION

Practice Instructions:

● Beginning on **C**, play five-finger pattern.

● Clap this rhythm repeatedly:

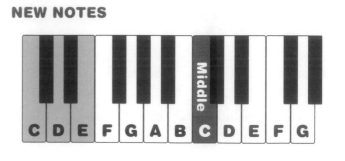

Invitation To A Picnic

● Play this piece first with the left hand alone.

Hungarian Play Tune

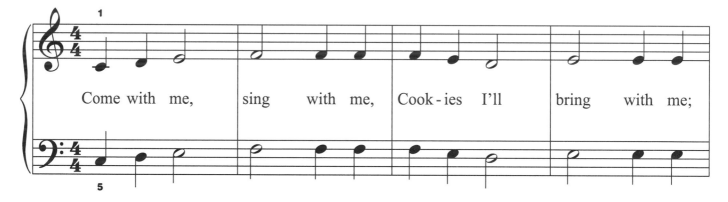

Come with me,   sing   with me,   Cook-ies I'll   bring   with me;

Join   the   fun,   ev - 'ry - one,   Play   in   the   sun   with me!

Teacher

> = **Accent Mark** (stress the note)

mf = **Mezzo Forte** = medium loud

Round Dance

Use **C** position (page 36).

Lively

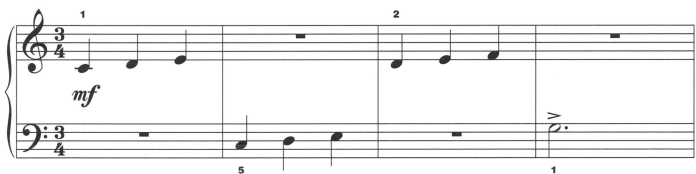

THE SLUR AS LEGATO MARK

The **slur** is a curved line placed over or under two or more notes.
It indicates the smooth, connected manner of playing called **legato**.

Legato an Italian word, means 'bound together'.
The notes bovund together by a **slur** are to be played
without any break or gap between the notes;
a depressed key is allowed to rise only when the next
key is depressed by another finger.

Cloudy Afternoon

Slowly

mf What a calm | af - ter-noon, | no-thing much to | do; | Cloud-y days,

mist - y skies, | make me feel so | blue, | *p* Make me feel so | blue.

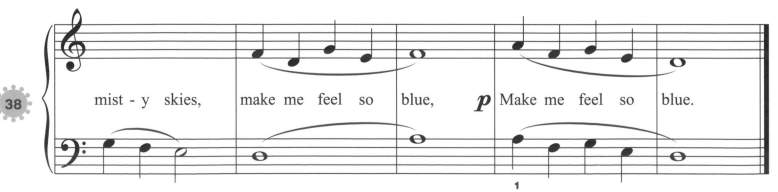

38

This sign is called a **crotchet rest**.
It indicates silence for one beat (one count).
It has the same time value as a **crotchet** (quarter-note)

Jump Tune

Use **C** position (page 36).

Merrily

f

TWO-NOTE SLURS

A **two-note slur** has two notes played legato, with a
graceful 'release' on the second note.

Playing a Two-Note Slur:

1. 'Fall' into the first key (from a high wrist to level with forearm)
letting the weight of the hand and arm 'sink' into the key.

2. Play the second note with legato touch and a graceful rise of the wrist.

3. Continue that motion as the arm and hand follow through, 'floating'
forward and releasing the key.

Flying

Rather slowly

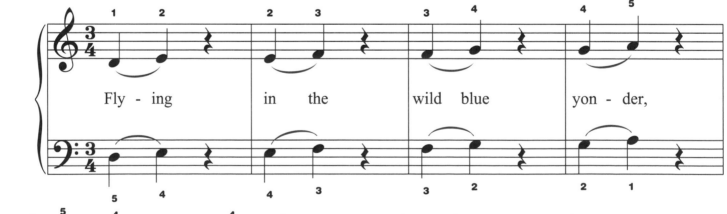

Fly - ing   in   the   wild   blue   yon - der,

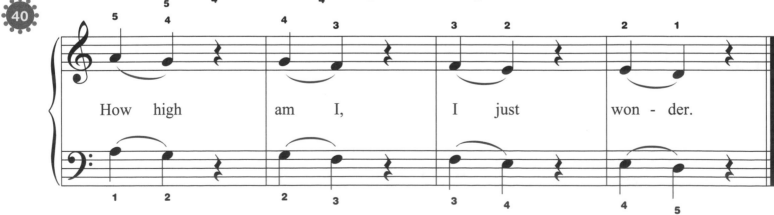

How   high   am   I,   I   just   won - der.

MELODIC & HARMONIC INTERVALS

Notes played one after another form a **melody**. The interval between two notes of a melody is called a melodic interval. Name these **melodic intervals**.

Two or more notes sounded together form **harmony**. The intervals between two notes sounded together is called a **harmonic interval**. Name these harmonic intervals:

This sign, a little bar sitting on the third line, is called a **minim rest** (half rest).

It indicates silence for two beats (two counts).

It has the same time value as a **minim** (half-note)

Marching Intervals

Walking tempo

f Up a se-cond, up a 3rd   up a 4th and   up a 5th;

Down a se-cond, down a 3rd,   up a 4th, now   left, right,   stop!

THE SLUR AS A PHRASE MARK

A group of notes connected by a slur often forms a melody unit called a **phrase**. **Phrases** are usually two to four **bars** in length.

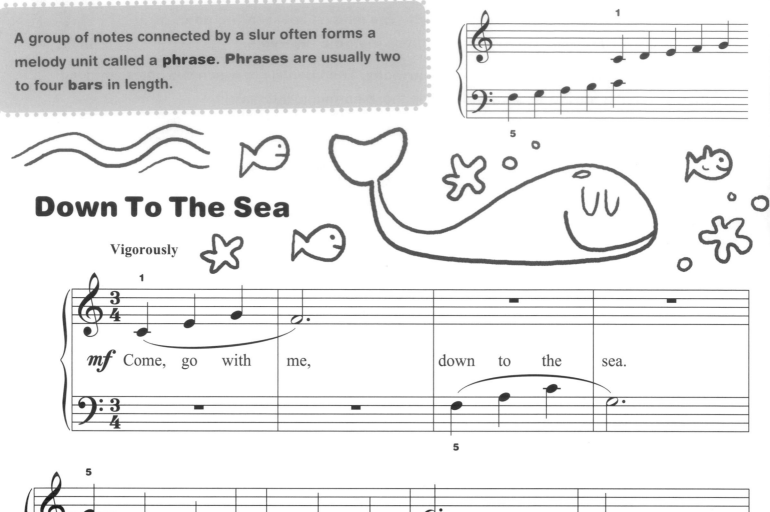

Down To The Sea

Vigorously

mf Come, go with me, down to the sea.

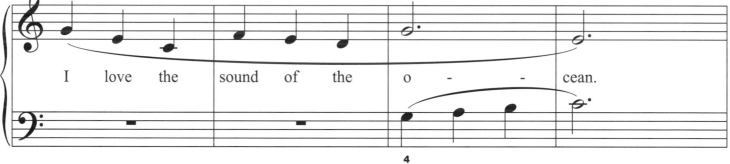

I love the sound of the o - - cean.

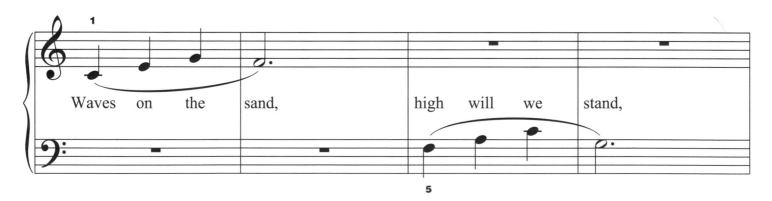

Waves on the sand, high will we stand,

Then we can watch them in mo - tion.

THE SHARP SIGN ♯

Placed in front of a note, the **sharp sign** ♯ *raises* that note to the nearest key to the right, black or white.

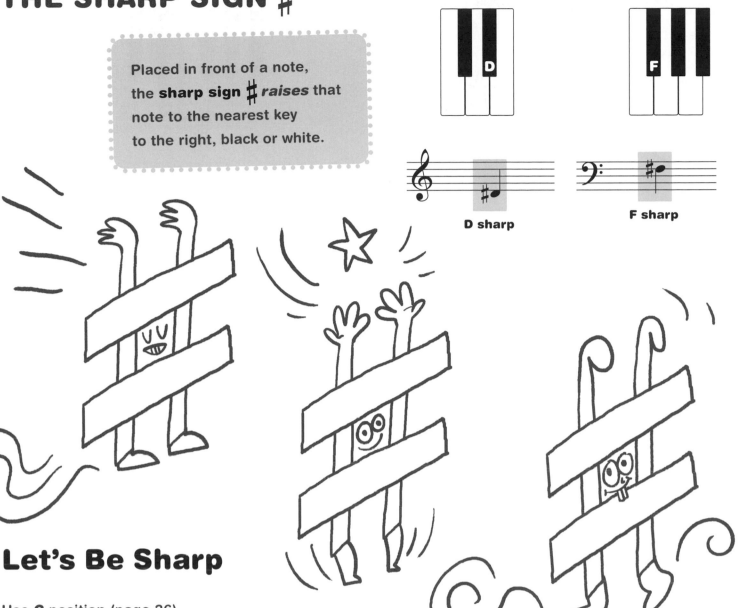

D♯

F♯

D sharp

F sharp

Let's Be Sharp

Use **C** position (page 36).

Moderately

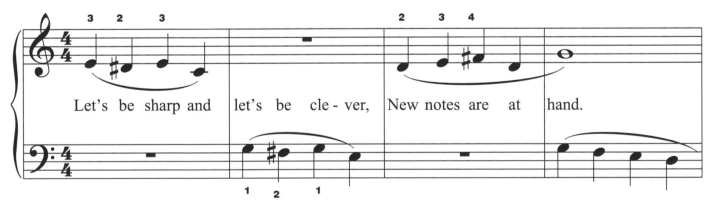

Let's be sharp and let's be cle - ver, New notes are at hand.

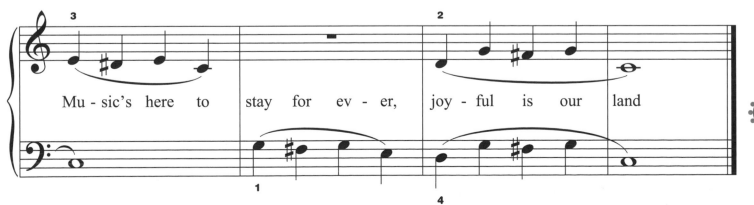

Mu - sic's here to stay for ev - er, joy - ful is our land

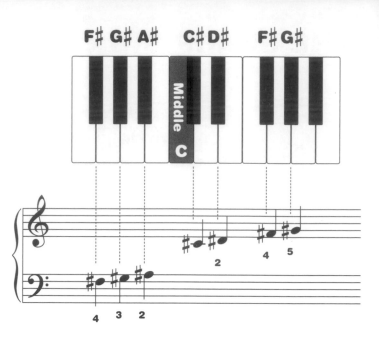

Lovely Evening Song

Gently moving

p There's a pale moon in the sky, Tem - ple

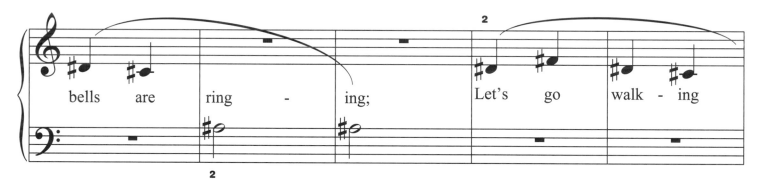

bells are ring - ing; Let's go walk - ing

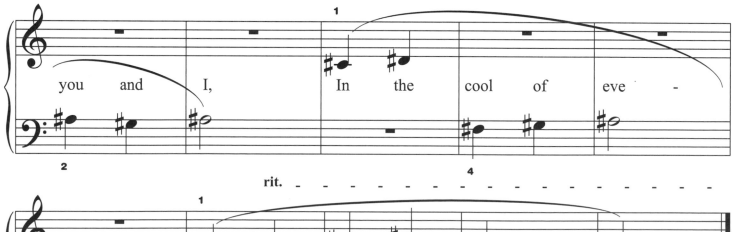

you and I, In the cool of eve -

rit.

- ning, What a love - ly eve - ning.

44

SKILL BUILDER: You can also play this piece on all white keys, starting on **F**.

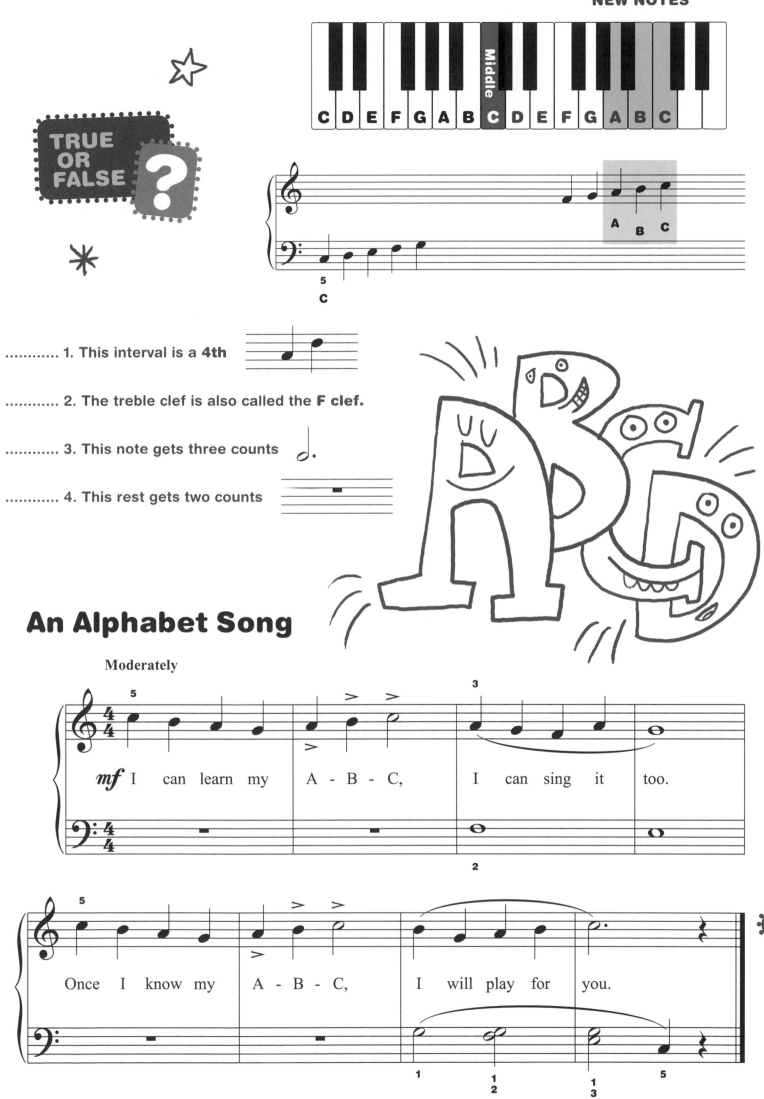

TRUE OR FALSE ?

.... 1. This interval is a **4th**

.... 2. The treble clef is also called the **F clef.**

.... 3. This note gets three counts

.... 4. This rest gets two counts

An Alphabet Song

Moderately

mf I can learn my A - B - C, I can sing it too.

Once I know my A - B - C, I will play for you.

45

Skating Partners

Smoothly moving

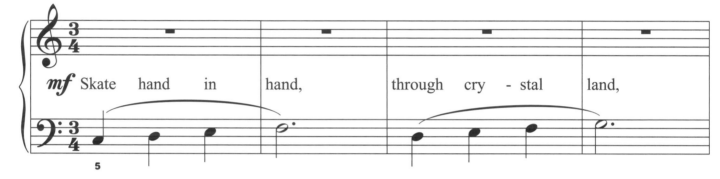

mf Skate hand in hand, through cry - stal land,

Skim - ming the edge of our fa - vour - ite pond.

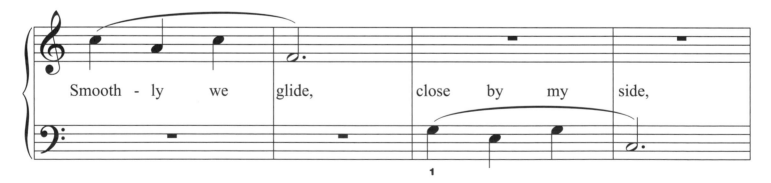

Smooth - ly we glide, close by my side,

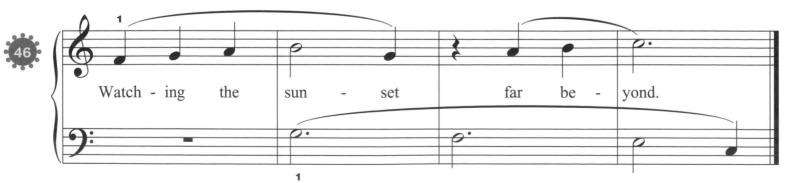

Watch - ing the sun - set far be - yond.

STACCATO

Staccato is the opposite of **legato**. A small dot above or below the notehead 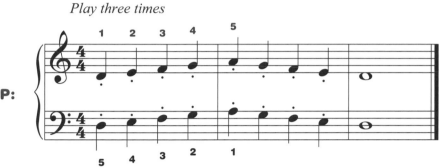 indicates that you should play in the short, detached manner called **staccato**. After striking the key, the finger bounces back, returning instantly to a raised position.

Play three times

WARM-UP:

Knock On Wood

Moderately

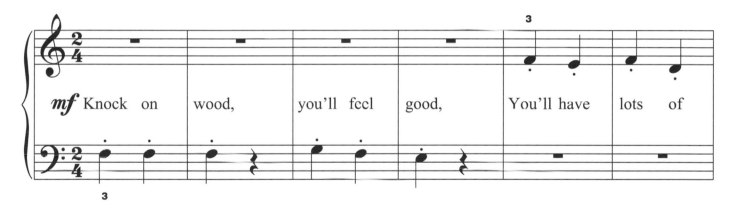

Knock on wood, you'll fccl good, You'll have lots of

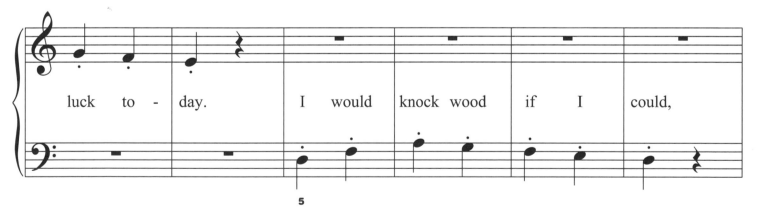

luck to - day.   I would knock wood if I could,

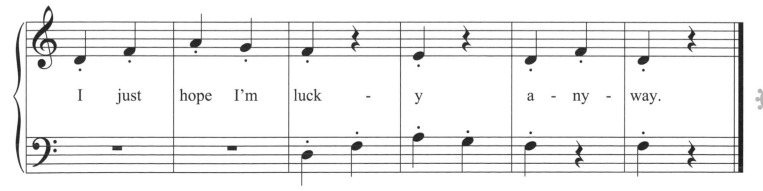

I just hope I'm luck - y a - ny - way.

47

● Observe the contrast between *staccato* and *legato* touches.

Cuckoo

Playfully

Folk Tune

Cuck - oo, cuck - oo, sing night and day.
Cuck - oo, cuck - oo, don't fly a - way.

Nev - er stop sing - ing joy you are bring - ing, Cuck - oo,

cuck - oo, why can't you stay? Cuck - oo, cuck - oo, cuck - oo.

THE FLAT SIGN ♭

Placed in front of a note, the **flat sign** ♭ *lowers* that note to the nearest key to the left, black or white.

E♭

E flat

A Touch Of Blue

Use **C** position (page 36).

Quite slowly

p Oh, boo - hoo! Think I have the flu.

mf It's a nice day, but I can't play, I'm so blue.

p

QUAVERS

 This is a **quaver** (eighth-note).
It looks like a **crotchet** (quarter-note) with a little flag.

 These are two **quavers**.
Two **quavers** are connected with a beam instead of being drawn with individual flags.

 Two **quavers** equal the time value of one **crotchet**, one count.

Count **quavers** this way:

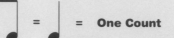

● Clap hands on every note and count aloud.

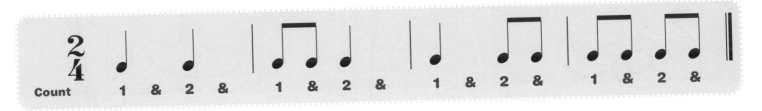

A Brief Stroll

Slow walking tempo

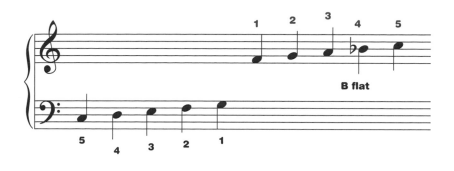

B flat

All the quavers here are connected by a beam. You play two quavers to one beat.

Dancing Quavers

Lively march tempo

Morning Call

Right hand position same as above.

Quite lively

Count   1 & 2 & 3 &   1 & 2 & 3 &   1 & 2 & 3 &   1 & 2 & 3

THE TIE

A **Tie** is a curved line connecting two neighbouring notes that are on the same line or in the same space. When two such notes are tied together we play only the first note and *hold the second note* without striking the key again.

- Remember the difference between a *slur* (the sign of *legato*) and a *tie*.

- Before playing the following piece mark every tie with a **T**.

Lullaby For A Rag Doll

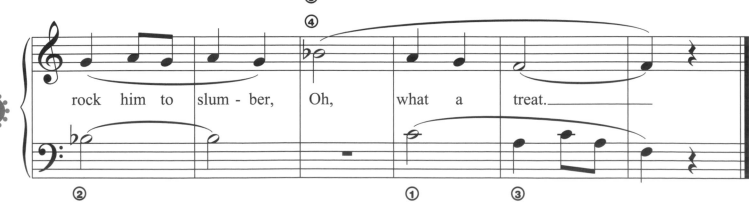

Slow and gentle rocking motion

p Rag doll, rag doll, sweet,_____

Cute from head to feet._____ Ev - 'ry night I

rock him to slum - ber, Oh, what a treat._____

A melody can start on any beat of the bar, not only on the first one.

NEW NOTE

'Cowboy Song' starts on the last beat of the bar, on count 'three.' This note will complete the missing beat in the last bar.

Cowboy Song

Gaily

mf We're up in the morn - ing ere break - ing of day, The

chuck wa - gon's bu - sy, the flap - jack's in play. The

herd is a - stir ov - er hill - side and vale, With the

night - ri - ders crowd - ing them in - to the trail.

MORE ABOUT SHARPS & FLATS

Sharps and flats alter not only the note in front of which they stand, but also all other notes on the same line or in the same space for the rest of that one bar (measure).

● Circle those notes which have to be raised or lowered, even though they do not have a sharp or flat in front of them.

Dear Wintertime

See hand position on next page.

Moderately

Folk Song

mf Snow fell to - day, Hope it will stay,

Then we can sled down the hill, Ride till we all take a spill,

Keep out the sun. Win - ter is fun!

54

SKILL BUILDER: You may also play this piece with all **F**s, instead of **F♯**s.

Did you change the mood?

Lightly Row

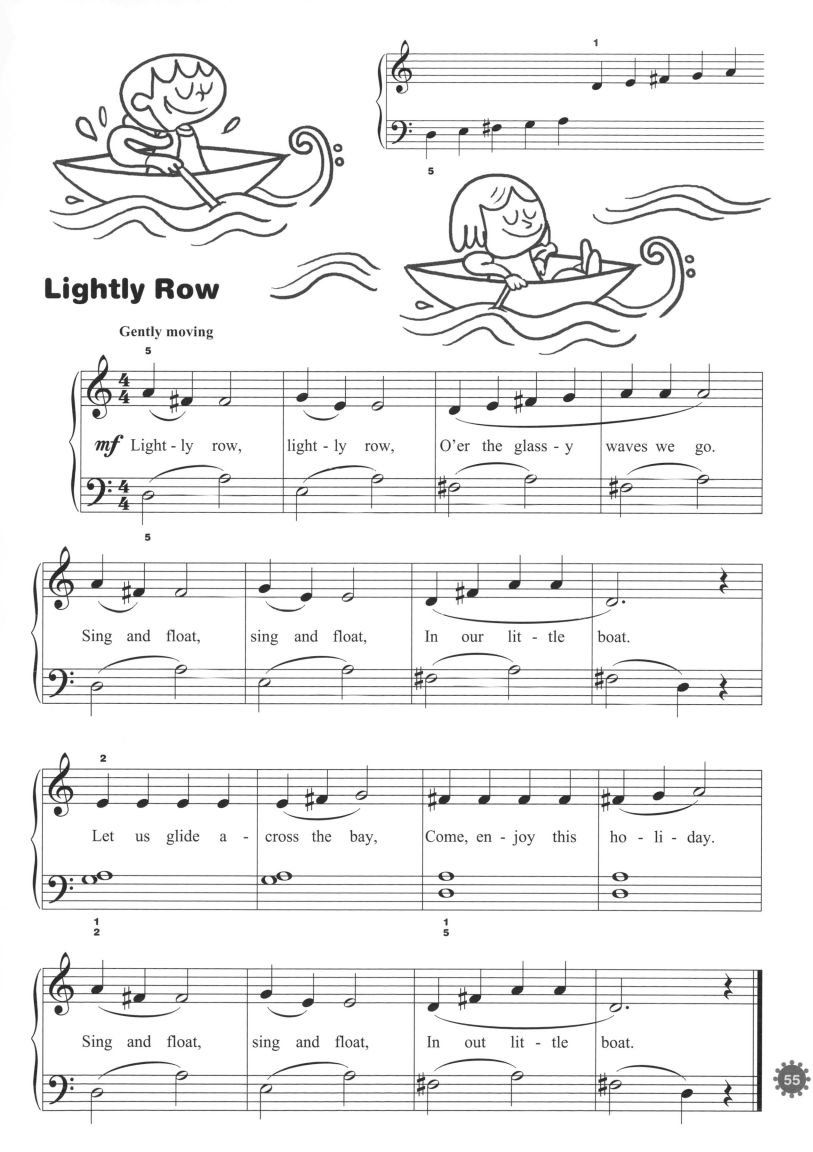

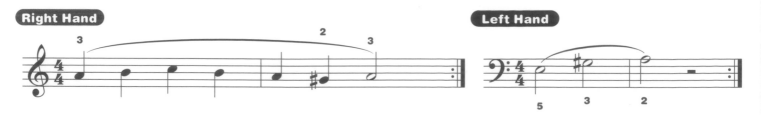

No School Today

Moderately slow

I'm in bed, no | school to - day, I'm | ail - ing
Tucked be - neath my | Gran-ny's quilt I'm | rest - ing,

I'm a - fraid my | health is real - ly | fail - ing.
Ice -cream cones is | all that I'm re - quest - ing.

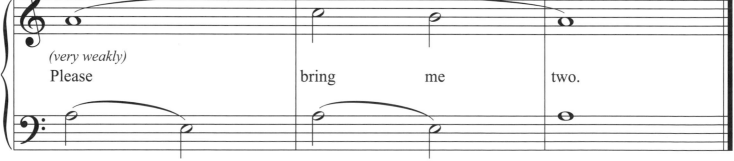

(very weakly)
Please | bring | me | two.

● **Write in the letter names of the notes.**

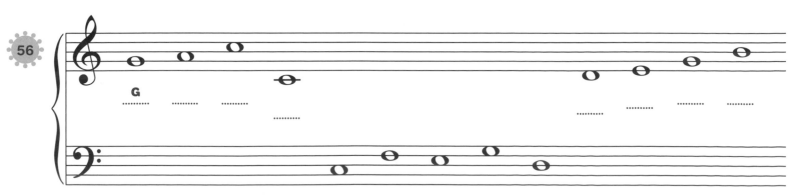

G

56

WARM-UP:

NEW NOTE

D

The Ballad Of Sad Sam

Moderately

Traditional Tunes

mf Once I loved my Au - ra Lee, Chased her night and day,
Now I love my Bon - nie lass, But she sailed a - way,

Lively

Bring back, bring back, Oh, bring back my

Bon - nie to me to me! Bring back,

bring back, Oh, bring back my Bon - nie to me, to me!

57

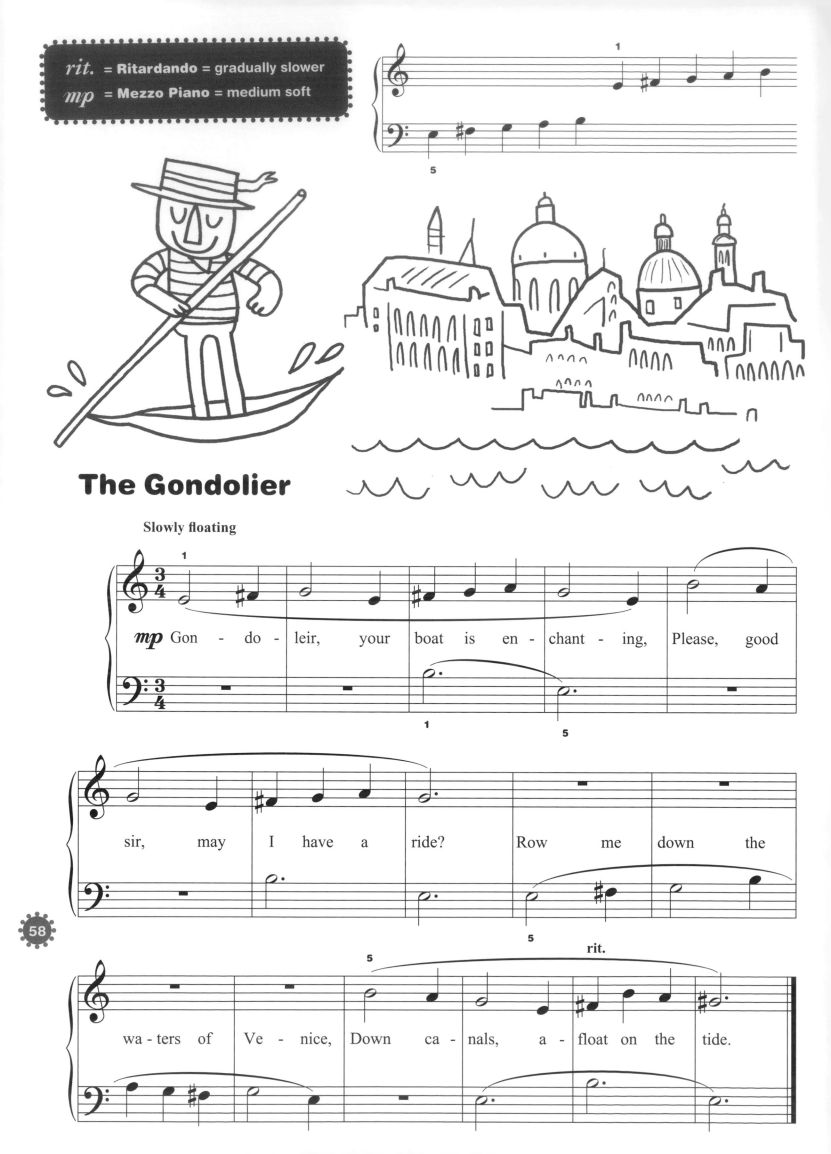

The Gondolier

Slowly floating

mp Gon - do - leir, your boat is en - chant - ing, Please, good

sir, may I have a ride? Row me down the

rit.

wa - ters of Ve - nice, Down ca - nals, a - float on the tide.

CHORDS

Three notes played together form a chord. There are various types of chords.

● Place your right hand on the keyboard in a five-finger position, with
the first finger on any white key. With fingers **1–3–5** strike three keys together
in doing so you play the simplest type of chord, called a **triad**.

This is how you find the C chord (for the left hand).

Also play an F chord and a G chord.

● With the right hand play a
C chord, an **F** chord, and a **G** chord.

Grandma

Play Tune

Moderato

f

mp

SKILL BUILDER: Play **C**, **F** and **G** chords, with each hand, in different octaves.

Sailors' Dance

Lively

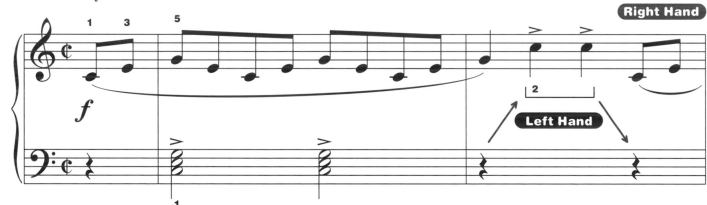

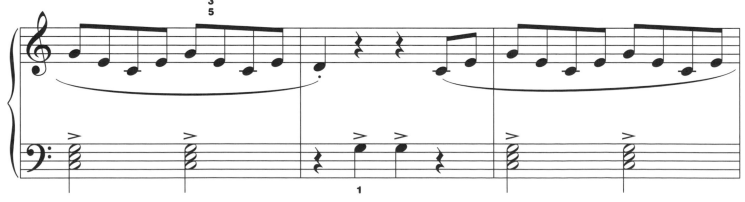

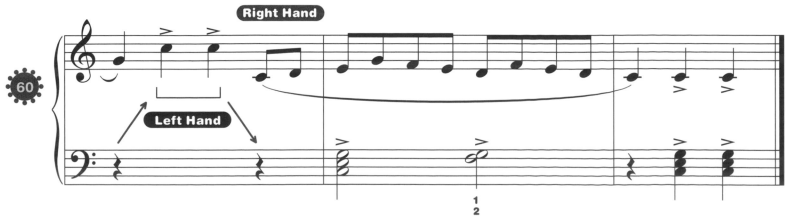

On The Playground

Lively

Hungarian Play Tune

Hop and skip and | jump and dip, And | 'round and | 'round we go!

Let us sing tra - la - la | Ding, dong, ding, tra - la - la,

You're the king, | tra - la - la - la, | I'm the queen, | tra - la - la!
I'm | | You're

61

WARM-UP:

● Name these intervals.

Valentine Greeting

In a slow, singing manner

Do you like me? You are en-tranc - ing, I just

wish that we could go danc - ing. Please don't let me pine,

Tell me you'll be mine. Will you be my sweet Va-len - tine?

.... 1. Each of these notes is a **D**.

.... 2. Two **quavers** ♫ have the same time value as one **crotchet**. ♩

.... 3. The opposite of **legato** is **staccato**.

.... 4. Each of these **intervals** is a **3rd**.

.... 5. A piece always starts on the first beat of a **bar (measure)**.

.... 6. This curved line is a **tie**.

.... 7. One of these **bars** has a beat missing.

.... 8. This is a **crotchet (quarter) rest**.

TRUE OR FALSE ?

DIRECTIONS OF STEMS

Notes on or above the middle (third) line have stems pointing down, touching the notehead on the left side.

Notes below the middle (third) line have stems pointing up, touching the notehead on the right side.

Draw stems for the following notes:

63

Tricks In Black And White

The **natural sign** ♮ cancels a **sharp** or a **flat**. When you see the sign in front of a note, you play the original white key.

Autumn Is Coming

Rather slow, moody

p Au - tumn is com - ing, clear and cold.
Leaves will be fall - ing, red and gold.

mf Wind sends them fly - ing, see them take wing,

rit.

p But they'll grow back and be green in the spring.

Right Hand 1   **Right Hand 2**   **Left Hand**

Raindrops On The Windowpane

Playfully moving

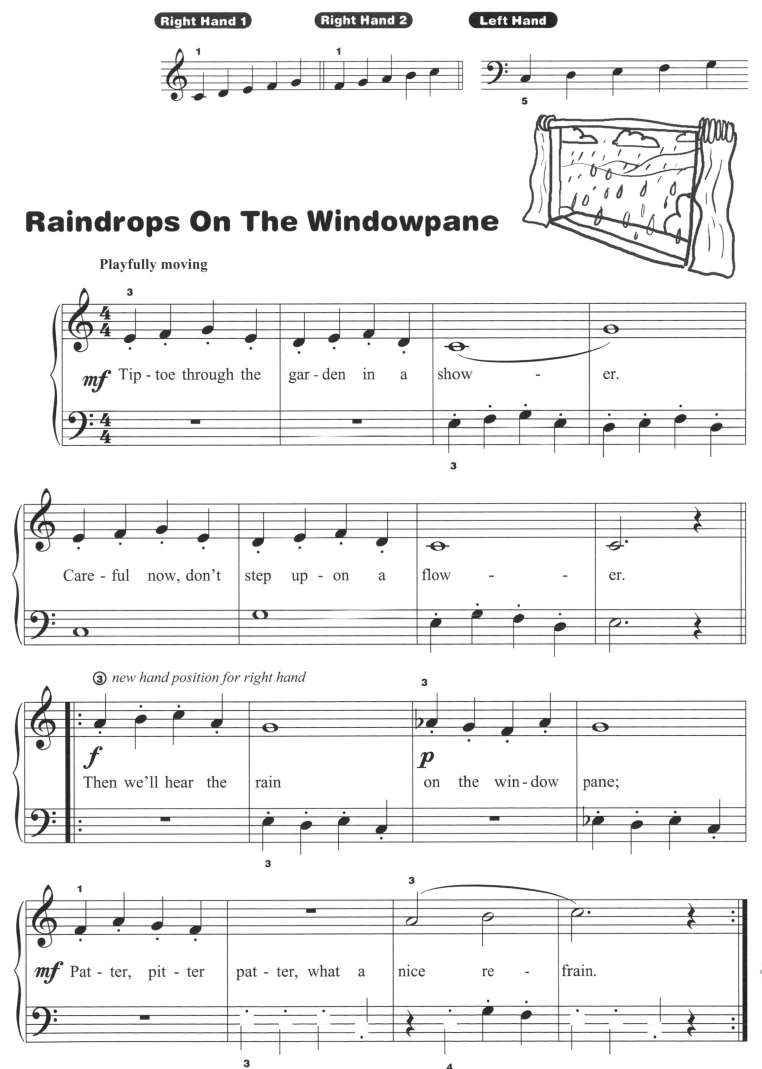

mf Tip - toe through the gar - den in a show - er.

Care - ful now, don't step up - on a flow - er.

③ *new hand position for right hand*

f Then we'll hear the rain   *p* on the win - dow pane;

mf Pat - ter, pit - ter pat - ter, what a nice re - frain.

Song Of Harmony

With fervor and warmth

f Let us give thanks for our loved ones and friends,

Change position

Let us be grate - ful that hope nev - er ends.

Change position

Peace be - tween peo - ple, yes, peace is the way.

Change position

If we keep try - ing we'll find it some day.

66

The Hurdy-Gurdy Man

Merrily

mf The Hur - dy - Gur - dy Man is down the street. He

is a jol - ly man you'd want to meet. His

mon - key dan - ces like an ac - ro - bat, and

then you drop your pen - ny in his hat.

67

may be repeated

PEDAL

The right pedal of the piano, when depressed, sustains the sound. Depress the pedal silently with the ball of your right foot (the heel stays on the floor).

Pedal Sign   Press   Hold   Lift

Recital Waltz

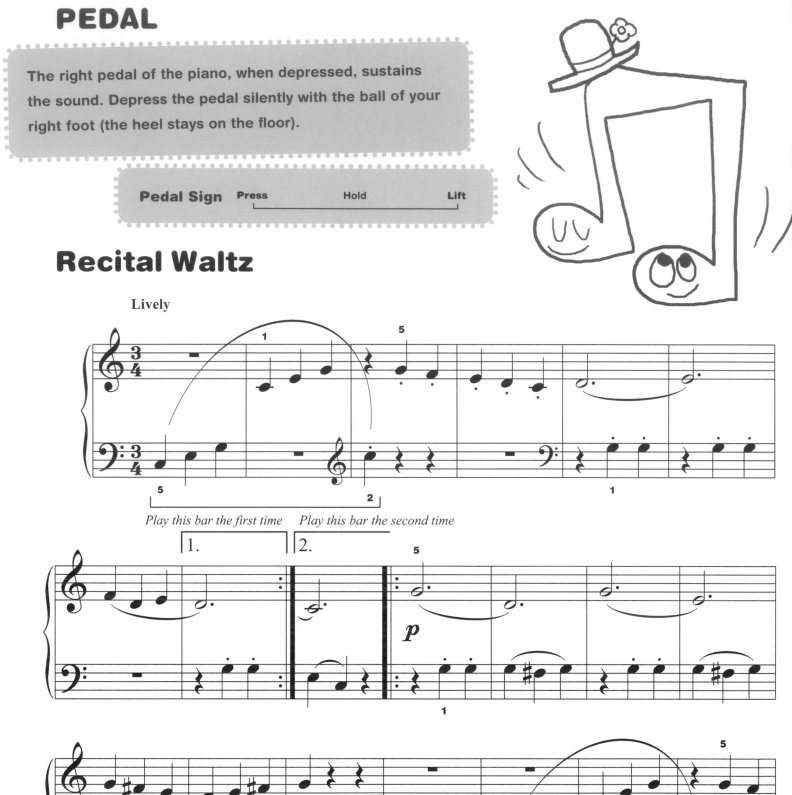

Play this bar the first time   *Play this bar the second time*

Junior Boogie

Moderately, with a strong beat

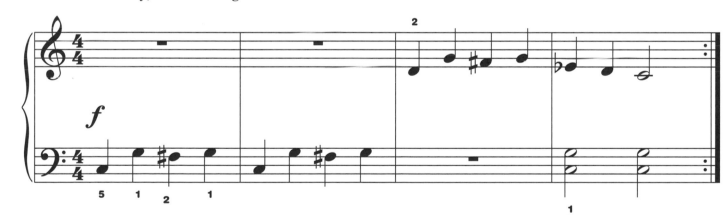

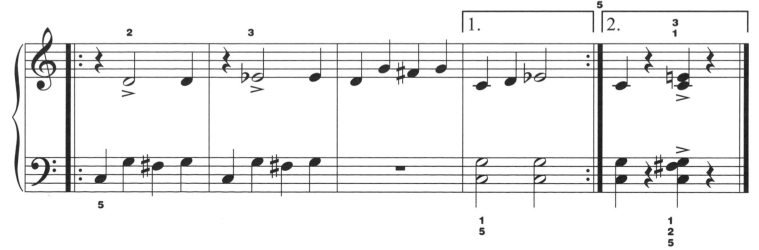

69

Crescendo or (*cres.*) (kre-shen-do) = gradually louder
Diminuendo or (*dim.*) (de-me-noo-en-do) = gradually softer

Campfire Song

Slowly, with feeling

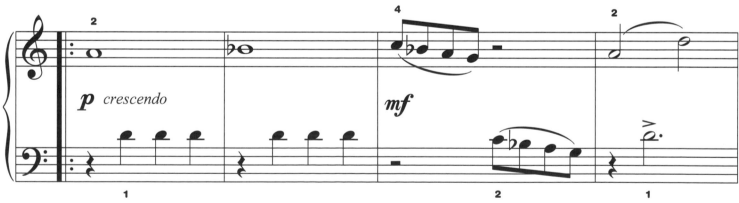

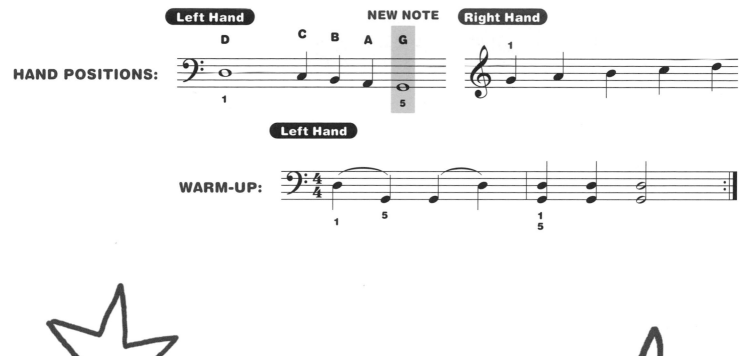

Left Hand D C B A **NEW NOTE** G **Right Hand** 1

Left Hand

WARM-UP:

New Adventures

Fine (end)

Repeat from start to Fine (with repetition)

71

Accent Mark: > stress the note.

Bar: the segment of music between two *Barlines* on the Stave.

Barlines: vertical lines dividing the stave into *bars* (measures).

Bass Clef: 𝄢 indicates lower notes on the stave, usually played by the left hand.

Chord: three notes played together.

Crescendo (*cresc.*): gradually louder.

Crotchet (*quarter-note*): ♩ (one count).

Diminuendo (*dim.*): gradually softer.

Dotted Minim (*half-note*): ♩. (three counts).

Double Barline: indicates the end of a piece.

f **forte:** loud.

F Clef: another name for the *Bass Clef*.

Fine: (*fee-nay*) the end.

Flat: ♭ lowers the note by a *semitone*.

Forte: loud.

G Clef: another name for the *Treble Clef*.

Grand Stave: a Treble Stave and a Bass Stave connected by a vertical line and a brace (bracket).

Interval: the distance between two notes.

Legato: smooth, connected manner of playing; marked by a *Slur*.

Letter names of the keys: A B C D E F G (the musical alphabet).

mf **mezzo forte:** medium loud.

Middle C: the white key just to the left of the two black keys in the middle of the keyboard.

Minim: ♩ (two counts).

mp **mezzo piano:** medium soft.

Natural Sign: ♮ cancels a *Sharp* or a *Flat*.

Note: a written symbol representing a *tone*.

Note Value: the duration or length of a *note*.

Octave: the interval of eight notes (both notes of the interval have the same letter name).

p *piano:* soft.

Pedal: part of the piano mechanism which, when depressed by the right foot, sustains the sound.

Phrase: a melody unit, usually two to four bars in length.

Piano: soft.

Quaver (*eighth-note*): ♪ (one half count).

Repeat Sign: :‖ means repeat the preceding section.

Rest Signs: 𝄽 Crotchet (quarter) rest. ▬ Minim (half) rest. ▬ Semibreve (whole) rest.

Rhythm: the sound pattern formed by a group of notes and pauses of various lengths.

Ritardando (*rit.*): gradually slower.

Semitone: the distance between one key and the very next key, black or white.

Semibreve (whole-note): 𝅝 (four counts).

Sharp: ♯ raises the note by a *semitone*.

Skip: when notes skip from a line to the next line, or from a space to the next space.

Slur: a curved line over or under a note group, indicating *Legato*.

Staccato (*stacc.*): a detached manner of playing, indicated by a dot over or under the note.

Step: when notes move stepwise from a space to the next line or from a line to the next space.

Tempo: the rate of speed in music.

Tie: a curved line connecting two neighbouring notes on the same line or in the same space.

Time Signature: two numbers written at the beginning of a piece, indicating the number of beats in a *bar* and the type of *note* that gets one count.

Treble Clef: 𝄞 indicates higher notes, usually played by the right hand.

Triad: a *chord* consisting of three notes; the root (lowest note), with the intervals of the 3rd and the 5th.